FENNEC FOXES

BY KRISTEN POPE

Published by The Child's World®
1980 Lookout Drive • Mankato, MN 56003-1705
800-599-READ • www.childsworld.com

Acknowledgments
The Child's World®: Mary Berendes, Publishing Director
Red Line Editorial: Editorial direction and production
The Design Lab: Design
Amnet: Production

Design Element: Shutterstock Images
Photographs ©: Hagit Berkovich/Shutterstock Images,
cover, 1, 10; Cat Downie/Shutterstock Images, 4; Petrov
Andrey/Shutterstock Images, 7; Shutterstock Images, 8, 16,
18; iStockphoto, 9, 19, 20–21, 22; Tobie Oosthuizen/
Shutterstock Images, 11; Vladimir Melnik/Shutterstock
Images, 12–13; Kiesel Und Stein/iStockphoto, 14–15

ISBN 9781631439681
LCCN 2014959638

Printed in the United States of America
Mankato, MN
July, 2015
PA02264

ABOUT THE AUTHOR

Kristen Pope is a writer and editor with years of experience working in national and state parks and museums. She has taught people of all ages about science and the environment, including coaxing reluctant insect lovers to pet Madagascar hissing cockroaches.

TABLE OF CONTENTS

CHAPTER ONE

DESERT DWELLERS 4

CHAPTER TWO

LOTS TO LEARN   10

CHAPTER THREE

WORKING TOGETHER 16

What You Can Do, 22

Glossary, 23

To Learn More, 24

Index, 24

DESERT DWELLERS

Fennec foxes are desert animals.

A tiny snout pops out of the sand. It is the nose of a fennec fox. The little fox is building its burrow.

The fennec fox is the smallest fox in the world. Most fennec foxes weigh only 2 or 3 pounds (0.9 to 1.4 kg). They are just 11 to 12 inches (27.9 to 30.5 cm) long.

They have very large ears that can grow 6 inches (15.2 cm) long! Fennec fox ears have a special job. They help keep the animal cool in the hot desert. The fox's blood comes close to the skin's surface on its ears. The ears have little fur to keep the heat in. This cools the blood down.

Keeping cool is important for fennec foxes. They live in the Sahara Desert. Other hot parts of northern Africa are part of their **habitat**, too. Fennec foxes are **nocturnal**. Being active at night helps them avoid the desert heat. Their long, thick fur is sandy in color. This keeps the foxes much cooler than they would be with dark-colored fur. Its length and thickness protects the foxes from the sun's heat. It also keeps them warm at night. Fennec fox tails have lots of fur. The tails help keep the foxes warm when curled around their bodies. Their tails have black tips, and so do the foxes' small snouts.

SPECIAL FEET

Fennec foxes have wide, furry feet. Their feet are like snowshoes. They help the foxes walk on top of the sand. The fur protects their feet from the burning hot sand. But their feet are like shovels, too. They help the foxes dig their burrows.

Fennec foxes live in northern Africa.

Fennec foxes look for food at night. They eat many different kinds of food. Sometimes they eat plants. Other times they eat **rodents**, birds, lizards, insects, and other animals. They eat bird eggs, too. Fennec foxes do not need to drink water regularly. They get water from the food they eat.

Fennec foxes are great jumpers. Adults can jump into the air more than 2 feet (0.6 m). Fennec foxes can jump more than 3 feet (0.9 m) across ground. Their sense of smell and hearing are also very good. They can hear beetles walking on sand. The foxes' jumping ability, combined with their hearing and smell, help them catch **prey**.

Small rodents, such as this jerboa, are fennec fox prey.

Fennec foxes live alone, in small groups, or pairs.

Fennec foxes live in burrows. They like to build their burrows at the base of sand dunes or hills. Fennec foxes usually live in small groups of ten or fewer animals. They can live in families, pairs, or alone. They make soft sounds or barks and squeaks to get one another's attention.

Baby fennec foxes are called cubs. They are usually born in late winter or early spring. Two to five cubs are born at a time. They are blind and helpless. But they are ready to be on their own by six to nine months old. Male and female foxes form pairs. They stay together their whole lives. In the wild, they typically live for ten years.

Fennec fox cubs can live on their own in less than a year.

CHAPTER TWO

LOTS TO LEARN

Scientists study wild fennec foxes to know how many there are.

Fennec foxes are not considered **threatened** or **endangered**.
But scientists say they do not know enough about the foxes.
They do not even know how many there are. For now, the
foxes are listed as "least concern." However, scientists know
the foxes are often trapped and sold. Some think the foxes

Jackals are excellent hunters that prey on fennec foxes.

could be considered threatened soon. More needs to be done to understand these animals and the threats to them.

Fennec foxes have several natural **predators**. Their small size makes them easy targets. Eagles and owls try to catch

HIDDEN FROM HUMANS

In the 1960s, scientists noticed fennec foxes were disappearing. They were missing from places in the Sahara Desert in Morocco, Africa. The places were close to where humans lived. Scientists realized fennec foxes do better when they live away from towns and villages.

them from the air. Jackals, hyenas, and pet dogs try to catch them on land. But catching the fast, **agile** foxes is difficult. They pop into their burrows at any sign of danger.

Humans are the biggest threat to fennec foxes. In areas where people live, **populations** of fennec foxes are in danger. The foxes often disappear due to human actions. This has happened in some parts of southern Morocco, Africa. Sometimes hunters kill the foxes for their fur. Some kill the

Villages in the Sahara Desert threaten fennec fox habitat.

foxes for food. Others kill them for sport.

People often capture fennec foxes to sell as pets. Buyers think the foxes are very cute. They want to keep them as pets. But living outside their wild habitat puts stress on the foxes. They can develop illnesses. They also keep many of their wild habits.

Some people capture fennec foxes to just show them off. They charge people to look at the foxes. Many tourists will pay to see an interesting animal. Some pay to hold one or have their picture taken with it as well.

Some people capture fennec foxes to make money.

CHAPTER THREE

WORKING TOGETHER

Some countries have passed laws to protect wild fennec foxes.

Few international laws exist to protect fennec foxes. But some nations, states, and local governments have passed laws to protect them.

Some African countries have laws to protect wild fennec foxes. Morocco, Algeria, Tunisia, and Egypt all do. Humans are moving into fennec fox habitat. They build homes and plant crops. Doing so takes up space in fennec fox habitat. This reduces the number of fennec foxes. The countries' laws protect fennec fox habitat. National parks and **conservation** areas provide a safe home to some

These countries have laws protecting wild fennec foxes.

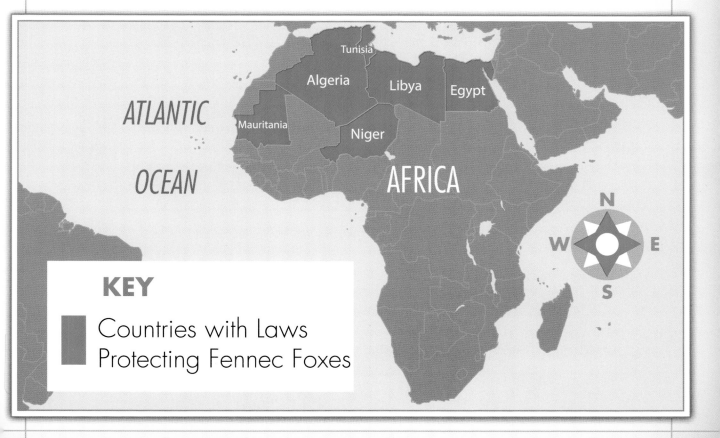

ATLANTIC

OCEAN

Tunisia

Algeria

Libya

Egypt

Mauritania

Niger

AFRICA

N

W   E

S

KEY

Countries with Laws Protecting Fennec Foxes

Fennec foxes do not make good pets.

of these animals. But many foxes are still being hunted, captured for display, or sold as pets. Other laws in some countries make it illegal to capture and sell the foxes.

WILD ANIMALS ARE NOT PETS

There are many Web sites about how to care for a pet fennec fox. But these wild animals are not good pets. Capturing them to sell lowers the number of wild fennec foxes. For these reasons, many people believe these animals are better off in the wild than in someone's house.

In the United States, fennec foxes are **exotic** animals. Each state and area has different rules about owning them. Texas and Wisconsin allow fennec foxes as pets. Delaware and Maine require people to have permits to have these animals as pets. Alaska and California ban fennec foxes as pets.

Scientists research fennec foxes in the desert of Tunisia.

Scientists are working to learn more about fennec foxes. They study fennec fox habitat. They learn how the animals behave in the wild. They watch how the foxes behave in groups. One place scientists are performing these studies is in Tunisia.

Some zoos display fennec foxes. When the foxes are in zoos, scientists can study them. Zoo visitors can learn about them, too. They can help spread the word about fennec foxes. Learning more about these animals often makes people want to help protect them.

Some zoos keep fennec foxes to study and show to visitors.

WHAT YOU CAN DO

- Never keep a fennec fox (or any other exotic animal) as a pet.

- Learn everything you can about fennec foxes.

- Tell everyone what you know about fennec foxes. Explain that they are better off wild than living as pets.

GLOSSARY

agile (AJ-il) When an animal is agile, it can move easily and quickly. Fennec foxes are agile.

conservation (kon-sur-VAY-shun) Conservation is the protection of animals, plants, and their habitats. Some conservation groups protect fennec fox habitat.

endangered (en-DANE-jerd) An endangered animal is in danger of dying out. Scientists are working to understand whether or not fennec foxes are endangered.

exotic (ig-ZAH-tik) Something exotic is very unusual, strange, or different. Some people keep fennec foxes as exotic pets.

habitat (HAB-uh-tat) A habitat is a place in nature where animals or plants live. The Sahara Desert is fennec fox habitat.

nocturnal (nak-TUR-nul) A nocturnal animal is one that is active at night. Fennec foxes are nocturnal.

populations (pop-yuh-LAY-shunz) Populations are groups of a certain kind of animal in a certain location. There are many different populations of fennec foxes.

predators (PRED-a-terz) Predators hunt, kill, and eat other animals. Fennec foxes have several predators in the wild.

prey (PRAY) Prey is an animal that other animals hunt and kill for food. Lizards are the prey of fennec foxes.

rodents (RO-dents) Rodents are small animals with fur and sharp teeth. Fennec foxes sometimes eat rodents.

threatened (THRET-und) An animal that is threatened is likely to become an endangered species. Scientists study fennec foxes to learn if they are threatened.

TO LEARN MORE

BOOKS

Aloian, Molly. *The Sahara Desert*. New York: Crabtree, 2013.

Gardner, Jane P. *Fennec Foxes*. New York: Bearport, 2014.

Scott, Traer. *Nocturne: Creatures of the Night*.
New York: Princeton Architectural Press, 2014.

WEB SITES

Visit our Web site for links about fennec foxes:
childsworld.com/links

Note to Parents, Teachers, and Librarians: We routinely verify our Web links to make sure they are safe and active sites. So encourage your readers to check them out!

INDEX

Algeria, 17

behavior, 4, 5, 7–8, 20

cubs, 9

Egypt, 17

fennec foxes as pets, 14, 18–19
food, 5, 6, 7

habitat, 14, 17, 20

illnesses, 14

laws protecting fennec foxes, 16–18

Morocco, 11, 12, 17

predators, 11–12

Sahara Desert, 5, 11

Tunisia, 17, 20

United States, 19

zoos, 20